Grow Your own Butterfly Farm

John Malam

Heinemann Library
Chicago, Illinois

www.heinemannraintree.com
Visit our website to find out more information about Heinemann-Raintree books.

To order:

☎ Phone 888-454-2279

💻 Visit www.heinemannraintree.com to browse our catalog and order online.

© 2012 Heinemann Library
an imprint of Capstone Global Library, LLC
Chicago, Illinois

Edited by Daniel Nunn, Rebecca Rissman, and Sian Smith
Designed by Philippa Jenkins
Picture research by Mica Brancic
Originated by Capstone Global Library Ltd
Printed and bound in China by Leo Paper Products Ltd

15 14 13 12 11
10 9 8 7 6 5 4 3 2 1

Library of Congress Cataloging-in-Publication Data
Malam, John, 1957-
    Grow your own butterfly farm / John Malam.
        p. cm.—(Grow it yourself!)
    Includes bibliographical references and index.
    ISBN 978-1-4329-5109-2 (hc)—ISBN 978-1-4329-5116-0 (pb) 1. Butterfly gardening—Juvenile literature. I. Title.
    QL544.6.M35 2012
    638'.5789—dc22   2010049834

Acknowledgments
The author and publisher are grateful to the following for permission to reproduce copyright material: Alamy pp. 13 (© Linda Kennedy), 16 (© Brian Hoffman), 21 (© LeighSmithImages), 25 (© Blickwinkel); Photolibrary pp. 15 (Polka Dot Images), 17 (Garden Picture Library/David Askham), 19 (Garden Picture Library/James Guilliam), 28 (Garden Picture Library/Kevin Dutton); Shutterstock pp. 4 (© Studio Foxy), 5 (© Elizabeth Spencer), 6 (© Ttphoto), 7 (© Tyler Olson), 8 (© Olga Altunina), 9 (© LilKar [Jakez]), 10 (© iladm [Olga Bogatyrenko]), 11 (© Antoine Beyeler), 12 (© Inc), 14 (© Margaret M Stewart), 18 (© Trombax), 20 (© Kitigan), 22 (© Vilax), 23 (© Andrew Park), 24 (© Marek Mierzejewski), 26 bottom (© Steve Byland), 26 top (© Lori Skelton), 27 bottom (© Sari ONeal), 27 top (© James Laurie), 29 (David Dohnal).

Cover photographs of various grasses blossoming on a meadow reproduced with permission of Shutterstock (© Sever180), and a monarch butterfly on a mass of white flowers reproduced with permission of Shutterstock (© Alex James Bramwell).

To find out about the author, visit his website:
www.johnmalam.co.uk

Some words are shown in bold, **like this**. You can find out what they mean by looking in the glossary.

Contents

Safety note:
Ask an adult to help you with
the activities in this book.

What Are Butterflies?

Butterflies are members of the **insect** family. They have brightly colored wings. Butterflies are insects that can fly. They only fly in the day, not at night.

This is a brimstone butterfly.

This monarch butterfly is drinking nectar. ▼

Butterflies feed on the **nectar** that is made by flowers. You can grow flowers that will attract butterflies. Many people enjoy watching butterflies in their yards.

What Are Wildflowers?

Wildflowers are flowers that grow in fields, meadows, and by roads. They grow wild, which means they grow where they want to. Butterflies like to feed on wildflowers.

Clover is a common wildflower.

Purple flowers attract a lot of butterflies.

There are many different wildflowers. Here are some you might know: thistle, buttercup, clover, dandelion, foxglove, milkweed, and coneflower.

Why Do We Need Butterflies?

Butterflies are good **insects** to have in a yard. When they land on a flower, specks of **pollen** stick to them. They take the pollen to other flowers.

pollen

Butterflies take pollen from flower to flower.

Flowers need pollen to make **fruit** and **seeds**. Insects that move pollen from one flower to another are called **pollinators**.

What Do Butterflies Eat?

Butterflies cannot chew food. Instead, they are drinkers. They drink water from puddles and ponds, and **nectar** from flowers. Nectar is a sugary liquid made by plants.

This butterfly is drinking water from a puddle.

proboscis

Butterflies use a feeding tube to drink through. This is called a **proboscis**. They push it into the nectar or water, then suck up the liquid.

Start Your Butterfly Garden

You can attract butterflies by growing wildflowers. You can grow them in a flower garden or in a large pot. Wildflowers like to be in the sunshine, so look for a sunny place to grow them.

Find a sunny place for your flowers.

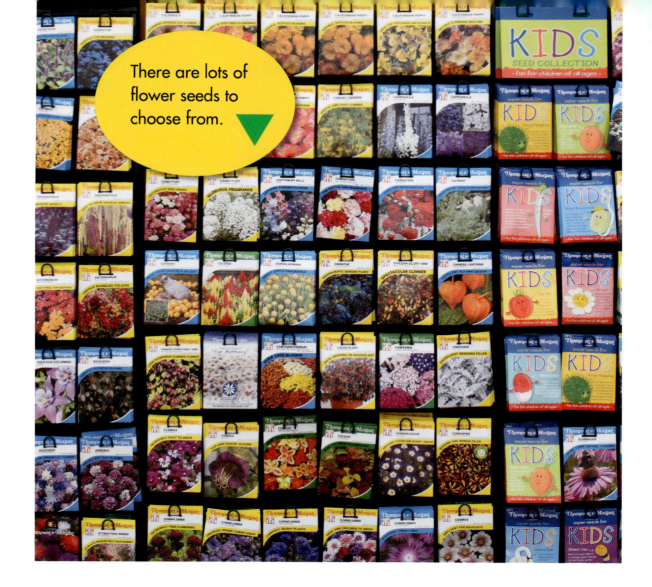

There are lots of flower seeds to choose from.

In the spring, buy a pack of wildflower **seeds**. Look for a pack that says the seeds will grow into plants that butterflies like.

13

Sow Wildflower Seeds

In early spring, clear the ground of weeds. Then, make a **seed bed** to **sow** your wildflower seeds in. Loosen the soil with a gardening fork. Break up any lumps. Rake it to make a fine, crumbly soil.

seed bed

Drag the rake across the soil.

Wildflower seeds can be tiny.

Pour a few seeds into your hand. Take little pinches of the seeds and **scatter** them across the seed bed. Use a gardening rake to mix the seeds into the soil. Sprinkle water over the soil with a watering can.

Cats and Birds—Keep Off!

Cats like **seed beds**. They dig up the fine soil, make a mess, and disturb the **seeds**. Birds peck the seeds and eat them.

Cats make a mess of seed beds.

To keep cats and birds away, cover the seeds
with a special cage or garden **netting**. You can take
this off when the seeds have grown into small plants.

Watering the Seed Bed

Keep the **seed bed** watered, specially in dry weather. Try not to let the soil dry out or the **seeds** will not grow. If it has been raining, the rain will have done the watering for you.

Sprinkle water on to the seed bed.

This tiny seedling has just been watered. ▶

After two or three weeks, look out for the tiny leaves of the first **seedlings**. It is often easier to spot them after the soil has been watered.

Add Some Marigolds

Butterflies like flowers that are brightly colored and stay open all day, such as marigolds. In the spring, plant nurseries and other stores sell trays of baby marigold plants.

These plants are in full flower.

There are a lot of marigolds in a tray.

Buy a tray of marigolds for your butterfly garden. Marigolds are shorter plants than most wildflowers, so put them in front of your wildflowers. This means you will be able to see them.

Watch Your Garden Grow

Wildflowers grow quickly in the warm months of spring and summer. Some, such as foxgloves and milkweed, will grow tall. Others are shorter, such as forget-me-knots.

Forget-me-knots are blue flowers.

flower buds

Foxgloves are tall flowers.

Look for the flower **buds**. Then watch them as they open into flowers over a day or two. Use a wildflower book to identify the flowers you have.

23

Butterflies have Landed!

When the flowers are open, look for butterflies landing on them. Butterflies like flowers that open flat out, so they have somewhere to stand.

Forget-me-knot flowers are a good shape for butterflies to land on.

This red admiral butterfly has landed on a buddleia.

What color flowers do the butterflies like the most? Look closely to see them drinking **nectar** through their feeding tubes.

Be a Butterfly Spotter

Look closely at the butterflies on the wildflowers. Look at the colors and patterns on their wings.

This is a swallowtail butterfly.

This is a fritillary butterfly.

This is a zebra butterfly.

This is a clouded sulphur butterfly.

Are lots of different kinds of butterflies coming to the flowers, or are they all the same kind? Use a butterfly book to identify the butterflies.

Be a Seed Saver

Toward the end of summer, the flowers will start to die. Don't pull them up! As they **wither** and dry, the flower heads make **seeds**.

Wildflowers make seeds for next year. ▶

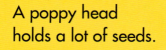

A poppy head holds a lot of seeds.

Shake the plants and the seeds will fall to the ground, ready to grow next year. Or you could pick off the dried flower heads. Keep them in a dry place, and you will have seeds to plant next year.

Glossary

buds flowers or leaves before they open

fruit part of a plant which can often be eaten as food. Fruit contains seeds.

insect small animal with six legs, no backbone, and a body divided into three parts

nectar sugary liquid made by plants

netting plastic net with holes in it

pollen tiny powdery grains made by flowers

pollinators animals, such as butterflies and bees, that move pollen from one flower to another

proboscis feeding tube of a butterfly

scatter to spread seeds across an area by throwing them

seed part of a plant that grows into a new plant

seed bed area of fine soil where seeds are sown

seedling baby plant

sow to plant a seed

wither to shrivel up

Find Out More

Books to read

Prischmann, Deirdre A. *Butterflies*. Bloomington, MN: Capstone, 2006.

Rabe, Tish. *My, Oh My— A Butterfly! (All About Butterflies)*. New York City: Random House, 2007.

Turnbull, Stephanie. *Caterpillars and Butterflies*. London: Usbourne Publishing, 2007.

Websites

http://butterflywebsite.com/butterflygardening.cfm

Find out about butterfly gardening and which butterflies are in your area on this Website.

http://www.thebutterflysite.com/

This Website has lots of information about butterflies, with picture galleries, fun activities, and much more.

Index